Trapping Time

Christopher White

Trapping Time

Copyright©2026 Christopher White

Hardcover ISBN: 978-1-7645017-0-5

Paperback ISBN: 978-1-7645017-1-2

Cover design by Christopher White

Published by Christopher White

Typesetting by Rack and Rune Publishing

rackandrune.com

Contents

Food for thought

Do you like your facts hard boiled or runny?
Your fears unfiltered or inflated by
self-raising doubt, prejudice and money.
Have you ever stopped to think and ask why?

If you asked for a steak and got a stack,
or that wasn't prepared like it should be,
do you send the plate with the waiter, back
and still expect to get the service free?

Nature has a bar tab that must be paid.
No matter how we wish the cheque away,
the tables cleared and cleaned. The mess we've made
another generation's After-Pay.

We tend to lacquer life with words. Mutton
dressed as lamb, cooked or covered in a glaze,
to make it more appealing. Whereupon,
like stunned mullets, we're drowning in a daze.

Get reality now or "Good to go"?
Perhaps an AI sauce to go with that.
The fraud exposed or tied up with a bow.
Lies and soda before the fizz goes flat.

Let's try not to order the same dish twice
overcomplicating the recipe.
Serve sashimi raw, whisky without ice.
Espresso double shot and sugar free.

Fame Game

Even though we see the show
and clap and smile, we do not know,
despite the tightly fitted robes,
is the emperor wearing clothes
or strutting in his underwear?

Life will never be the same
when everybody knows your name.
Feeling they can stop and stare,
Truth or dare, no-one cares.
Every dog will have its day.

Performers on a public stage
Come and go. Turn the page
or 15 minutes after curtains fall
the crowd has gone or can't recall.
Fleeting is the game of fame.

Nothing here is here to stay.
Fame, like fortune, slips away.
It came and went. Fame foregone,
all I can rely upon
are the minutes of this day
I have left to spend with you.

Gate Pass

Prisons do not all have bars,
and not all walls are brick,
when pain and incapacities
incarcerate the sick.

Trapped inside this dungeon
invariably we find
the chains that bind most tightly
are anchored in the mind.

There may not be an answer yet.
No cure or a key,
to unlock these chains and shackles.
Setting those who suffer free.

Precious then the moment,
unpardoned on parole,
when wellness felt like freedom
and a Gate Pass for the soul.

The Mirror Maze

We walk within a mirror maze.
The images we see
amuse us as we take our turn.
What hides the passage free
are reflections of ourselves.
Too many lose their way,
misled by mirrors in our minds
that tempt us all to stray.

Confused are they who come to some
abrupt and blind dead end
yet faithful to appearances
in fantasy defend
that which another says they see
must be a measure true
of whom you are and what you're worth
shining back at you.

But mirrors can be made to make
us seem what we are not.
They tell us we possess the things
we want and haven't got
and those who see themselves
through another person's eyes
will see their worth with opinion, change
and still be less than wise.

It's not until we see beyond
the boundary of our face
that we make sense of what we see,
and wayward steps retrace.
For when our eyes no longer
see reflections, we begin
to see what lies behind the mask.
We find the wealth within.

Yet though none can forever pass
a point of no return,
answers only come to those
who asks questions. We can learn
if we lose our way within this maze
and images confound,
to not look in the mirror
but more closely at the ground.

For there a path, the track well worn,
lies etched upon the floor
whereon the wise in days gone by
had passed along before.
So, pay no head to what you see
reflected round about.
There is a path from chaos
that with faith will lead you out.

Run

The clock on the wall has been slow for years.
Close enough to not condemn,
but behind the times or ahead of them,
it runs.

When there is nothing left to keep us here.
The future's bright and the past is black.
Facing forward, don't look back
and run.

Anticipation overcoming fear
and expectations to be met.
What if Romeo and Juliette
had run?

If we make a stand and stay and choose
to play the game with what we've got,
bet the house and stake the lot.
Or run

when the more we play the more we lose.
Cash our chips in, cut the loss.
A rolling stone doesn't gather moss.
So run.

With the baying crowds in hot pursuit.
Debt collectors at the door
and everybody wanting more.
Just run.

If standing still makes no sense to you
and there's another place to be,
the only thing that makes sense to me
is run.

When the sign says "Stop", just drive on through.
Hand in hand and side by side.
Strap in tight for the wild ride
we run.

The Best Thing

The best things in life are not things.
The best things in life don't get old.
Despite all the pleasure and joy that it brings
the best thing in life can't be sold.

It isn't a path or a journey or way.
But there isn't a moment to lose
when it still has a price. And the price that we pay
is something we all get to choose
to spend. It's not free. Even though we forget
or distracted, ignore passing by.
The best thing in life is a gift that we get
from the moment we're born till we die.

The best thing in life are moments like these.
The best thing in my life it's true
are the moments I have and mean most to me.
It's the time that I spend here with you.

Thinking

Ticking. Ticking.
I can hear the old clock ticking
and like the thoughts that I am thinking
in the silence both seem loud.

While logic, wheels of logic
turn, and thoughts and hands keep pace.
Paths that both in sequence trace
are neither simple nor profound.

But revolving keep evolving.
From a thought, a new thought born.
We're to new horizons drawn
or precedent recall

within the realm of reason.
Responses varied and diverse
are unceasing in their search
for answers. Some are found

while most remain unsolved.
Failure does not mean defeat.
Logic's metronomic beat
knows no other sound.

Thoughts turn in a full circle
to the point where once begun.
Hands divergent rejoin one.
Like the clock upon the wall
Ticking.

This Land Their Voice

Let me first paint you a landscape. With words. About this land
where the waves are never-ending, and pine trees proudly stand.
When islands in three oceans forged this southern nation and
ringed in gold, was boldly crowned by wind-blown sun-bleached sand.

Where quanta of each crystal quartz, first in a breaker borne
are thrown back against the shores from whence they once were torn
to weave its crown from weathered rock. Wild waters are the host
in which the beach was born and cast in fury to the coast.

A land where tides hide treasures from the deep, a shell, a pearl
from the vast eternal ocean where endless breakers curl
and the pounding of the surf upon the seashore, like a heart,
is the essence of a country sea and time have set apart.

A country changing colour. Where the red relentless ray
turns newborn buds that once were green a gaunt and lifeless grey.
And tempest tossed the seagulls soar in dark and stormy skies
to guard the windswept whiteness with their eerie piercing cries.

Or the waves' incessant rhythms paint alternating hues
of icy cold foreboding greens and iridescent blues
while the foam, in white rebellion, is seething to be free
but cannot cut its shackles to the unrepenting sea.

Where from the surf an onshore breeze brings sweetly to the nose
the salty scent of sea-spray. And the sand between your toes
like softly sifted grains of gold are quick in their cascade
to undermine and then erase the mark your passing made.

A land of ancient legend. Where flowing in her veins
is the spirit of First Nation sons and daughters. What remains
of an era long forgotten, a dreamtime come and gone,
is their voice. Where myth and magic in the silence linger on.

The lichen covered rockface is red on black beside
a rock-pool, as a remnant of the last receding tide,
that holds a mirror image of the sun. And sea and sand
combine to paint the emblem of the owners of this land.

Time is a thief

Time is a thief and
as the seconds pass events
are easily forgotten.
Lost, unless we have the sense
to lock the fleeting moments
of these precious passing days
within a verse or sentence.
Captured in a phrase
before it slips into the abyss
of the unremembered.

So I write. Not for another
when not many will agree
with how I think and what I say.
I write these lines for me.
To keep account of what occurred
and how my life has changed.
To try and snare the seconds
of existence. And I aim
to paint as any artist
captures mood in form and line,
with words. To conjure pictures
in the corner of my mind
of places, people, feelings,
things I've thought and could not say.

Uniquely felt for the first time,
wrote down and put away,
to guard against these minutes
as they march. To then one day
reread and recollect that
once I felt a certain way
or had a certain thought.
And in comparing Now and Then,
lessons learned are relearned
when my memories live again.

Passing time

Passing time at Wylie's Baths
The waves beyond a pond of glass
Ripples as the swimmers pass
Back and forth. Came and went.

Floating then in Gordon's Bay.
Coloured fish dart and play
Among the rocks and fronds that sway.
Tassels that the tides torment.

Strolling in Centennial Park
Bikes and horses kept apart
By lines and lanes of trees and cars.
Parades of people. A movement

that merrily around it goes.
Time is life. We ebb and flow
And in that moment come to know
That passing time is time well spent.

An Aussie Blessing

There's always another bus on the road,
There's always another train on the track.
Travelling with friends may lighten the load,
But keep looking forward and don't look back.
Don't let the fear of failure define you
Remorse is the route to a darker place.
As much as you can always design to
Sit at the front with the sun in your face.
Then your shadows will all fall behind you.
Regret is a ghost that cannot return
If setbacks serve to simply remind you
Those were the lessons you needed to learn.
Our stories change from the moment they start.
Write your next chapter with a happy heart.

Trapping time

Entries in the Archibald
are painted portraits on a wall.
The famous faces we recall
do not really tell us all
we need to know about who they are
or what they did or how they think.

Lines of paint capture light and colour.
I use paper, pen and ink
trapping time between these lines.

Spinnerets inside my head
like a spider's golden web,
spun with words of silk instead.
Catching in its sticky thread
everything I did and said.
Immobilised. Unfrozen when
the moment is relived reread.

More or less

Choice is chance. Compelled to take it,
See the goal and try to make it.
Set a record just to break it.
Get outplayed and try to fake it.

Ever stop to wonder why
a lie begets another lie.
As quicksand sucks the more we try
to grasp at things as they fly by

this gets worse the more we fight it.
Vanity ablaze despite it
burning us because we light it.
Lost the plot and to re-write it,

try to float when we are sinking.
Have a drink, but don't keep drinking.
Think, but don't let overthinking
interfere and mask an inkling

of the meaning in the mess.
In pursuit of happiness,
none of it makes sense, unless
less is more and more is less.

Whatever may have come before,
Most of it we can ignore.
The poor are rich, the rich are poor
when more is less and less is more.

Nine Archers

They dress in skin-tight thermals
and threadbare mismatched socks
when "hands across the boat"
chirps the ever cheerful cox
and the morning lights first feeble rays,
in search of day, pierce through
the rising mist. A city sleeps;
the sun will greet this crew.

None fear the cold discomfort.
They're immune now to its bite
and ensuing work will warm them.
While in the morning light
still waters form a mirror.
In the river they reflect
to form a double image
that they practice to perfect.

The puddles pass behind the boat
until the smallest swirls
are swallowed in the stillness
and as the dawn unfurls
the only imperfection
on the surface of the lake
is a tiny ripple, testament
to this living quarrel's wake.

Backs brace like an archers bow.
With grace and tensile ease
this bolt of eight young athletes
is launched in harmonies
of co-ordinated movement.
The shell runs straight and true
when eight combine their power
and become as one a crew.

With every act a copy of
the pattern set by Stroke.
Muscles gnarled and knotted
strain beneath their yoke
and sitting back, with smooth release,
unleash the force applied.
In synchrony blades feather
when they're rolled onto their side.

To the rhythm of the Stroke.
The oar, a sweeping swallow,
skims the lake; at equal height
another seven follow.
With elegant precision
that is felt more than is seen
eight feathered blades in unison
leave the water clean.

When level hands are balancing
while easing down the Slide
beneath the boat the water sings.
Recovering, they glide.
Angles close until force compressed,
recoiled at the Catch
without a wasted movement
that is sprung with sharp dispatch.

The clip of eight bright blades
resounds as one around the bay
when the oars lock in united
to send her on her way.
Accelerating rapidly
the boats alacrity
belies the strength required
and how painful that can be.

For they train to race. They train to win
and their patience is repaid
when they come before the starter's gun.
In flight the flashing blade
needs quick acceleration
and a rate of forty two
commands complete control
of every trained and tense sinew.

They race two thousand meters
in five minutes. At these speeds
equal strength and stamina
is what each oarsman needs.
For when the hungry bows divide
and scythe in two the course
the fuel to feed the fury
is the maximum of force.

Imagine if you can the pace
as six crews race and how
with the finish fast approaching
your opponents push their bow
half a length ahead.
The coxswain makes a final call
to lift the rating higher,
and straining one and all

They lunge toward the finish line
oblivious to pain
with nothing left to lose
and much in winning gain.
A merciful exhaustion
overwhelms at races end
as agonising breath and
tired weariness descend.

The winner's quick recovery,
their weariness soon past,
will leave unwanted pain the fate
of those who are outclassed.
To the victor goes the honour
while the vanquished weakly toss
their vessel from the water
and bear it like a cross.

The burden weighs on shoulders
and their faces show dismay
accepting the defeat.
They know there is no other way
except to train and toil
on the water every dawn.
A morning homage to the sun
until success is born.

So if you ever rise
before the birds and chance to see
nine archers launch their quarrel,
to pierce serenity,
it's a daily rite repeated
and a price that they will pay
in pursuit of their perfection,
and to race another day.

Zero Sum

At first, we learn to crawl
and walk before we run.
To stand before the fall
we fell before we won.
The win, when we have lost
was someone else's win.
Whatever it may cost,
the margin wafer thin.

We step or else we stop.
We either will or won't
rise before we drop
or do before we don't.
We carry what we keep.
Alone till we belong.
Awake until asleep.
Weak until we're strong.

We're strong until we crack
and wrong until we're right.
Its white unless its black
playing black and white.
One plus one was two.
Until it became three.
Others said so too.
Our unsatiety

a hunger we cannot
easily appease.
We want more than we've got.
We take more as we please
and call it growth instead.
Unrestrained, it meant
the buffers have been bled
and tolerances spent.

Possessions packed in bags
Are slipping from our grip.
We swam between the flags
Until there was a rip.
Life is zero sum.
In twenty twenty-four
every year to come
is hotter than before.

Thresholds have been met.
Rivers running dry
until they're very wet
and overflow. The sky,
a precious biosphere,
we did not protect.
We didn't want to hear.
What did we expect?

None of this is new.
She has seen it all before.
Her biofilm askew,
Gaia knows the score.
The Human Race is run
by rules we try to bend
before it had begun.
All Life on Earth will end.

To stop, is to begin.
As long as Life persists
the same end game wherein
it ends if it exists.
Cosmic incarnations
alert and aware we
bear witness to creation's
dance with entropy.

One thing

One chance is all I'll ever need
to turn a loss into a win,
To learn the lesson locked therein
or failing that, at least One friend
who cares and watches out for me.
A sounding board so I can cope.
One word that turns anguish to hope.
One minute more for me to mend
this tattered sail in a stormy sea.
Something to take the pain away.
One wink to say, "It'll be Ok!"
when I know it's not.
                              It will depend
on what the next setback will be.
One meal that doesn't go straight through.
One breath so I can laugh with you.
To pick my clothes up off the floor.
One day that I can move once more.
That I can walk and turn and bend.
One wish. That my identity,
and fierce held independence are
linked, having fought to come this far,
Whatever may or could happen,
One family to be with me when,
my race is run. This journey's end.

Never say No.

The clock is ticking. Even though
The more I try the worse I go
And it is generally agreed
Less done in haste would increase speed,
we don't know what tomorrow brings.
Nothing's over 'til the fat lady sings.

The only way that I can cope
is roll the dice again and hope
that lady luck will smile my way.
Tomorrow is another day.
The more I learn the less I know.
Never say never and never say no.

The Magic of Xmas

The magic of sharing is
A pleasure shared is a treasure doubled
And trouble shared is a burden halved.

The magic of caring is
Guardians grow by being and doing
And those they care for are safe and secure.

The magic of giving is
The gift is greater when the givers get
more in return than was given away.

The magic of Xmas is
We share, we care and we love to give
when to give is to love.